Die Geschichten vom Brownstone: Eine Anthologie von Kurzgeschichten für Englischlerner

Artici English

Published by Artici English, 2024.

While every precaution has been taken in the preparation of this book, the publisher assumes no responsibility for errors or omissions, or for damages resulting from the use of the information contained herein.

DIE GESCHICHTEN VOM BROWNSTONE: EINE ANTHOLOGIE VON KURZGESCHICHTEN FÜR ENGLISCHLERNER

First edition. April 29, 2024.

Copyright © 2024 Artici English.

ISBN: 979-8224505388

Written by Artici English.

Inhaltsverzeichnis

The Enigmatic Elevator

IN THE HEART OF BUSTLING New York City, amidst the towering skyscrapers that scrape the clouds, there stood a peculiar building known as "The Enigma Tower." It was a structure that seemed to defy the laws of architectural logic, its sleek facade adorned with mysterious symbols etched in gold. But it wasn't the exterior that intrigued the city dwellers; it was what lay hidden within—the enigmatic elevator.

Now, this elevator was no ordinary contraption. It was said to possess mystical powers, capable of transporting its passengers not just between floors but through time and space itself. Many tales circulated about the strange occurrences within its metallic confines, whispers of individuals who entered and emerged forever changed.

On a dreary Tuesday afternoon, a young boy named Tommy found himself standing before the entrance to The Enigma Tower. He had heard the rumors, the tantalizing tales of adventure and mystery that awaited those brave enough to step inside. With a heart full of curiosity and a mind ablaze with wonder, Tommy pushed open the ornate doors and stepped into the lobby.

The interior was just as grandiose as the exterior, with marble floors that gleamed under the soft glow of chandeliers. Tommy approached the elevator cautiously, his eyes wide with anticipation. As he reached out to press the call button, a voice spoke from behind him.

"Are you looking for a bit of excitement, young lad?"

Tommy turned to see an old man, dressed in a tattered coat and sporting a mischievous grin.

"Who are you?" Tommy asked, his voice trembling with excitement.

The old man chuckled. "Some call me the Keeper of Secrets, others simply know me as Jack. But enough about me, are you ready to embark on a journey unlike any other?"

Tommy nodded eagerly, his heart pounding in his chest. Without another word, Jack gestured towards the elevator, and Tommy stepped inside, the doors closing behind him with a soft hiss.

As the elevator began to ascend, Tommy felt a strange sensation wash over him, like a whirlwind of emotions swirling around in his mind. The walls of the elevator seemed to shimmer and warp, morphing into scenes from a distant past.

He found himself standing in the bustling streets of 1920s New York, surrounded by flappers and gangsters. The air was thick with the sounds of jazz music and the scent of prohibition-era speakeasies. Tommy watched in awe as the city transformed before his eyes, a kaleidoscope of colors and cultures.

But just as quickly as it had begun, the scene shifted once more. Now, Tommy found himself in a futuristic metropolis, where flying cars zipped through the air and robots roamed the streets. He marveled at the technological wonders that surrounded him, his eyes wide with wonder.

With each floor they passed, Tommy's sense of wonder grew, his thirst for adventure unquenchable. It was as if The Enigma Tower had become a portal to a thousand different worlds, each more fantastical than the last.

Finally, after what felt like an eternity, the elevator came to a stop, and the doors slid open to reveal a sight unlike any other. Tommy stepped out into a lush paradise, where emerald forests stretched as far as the eye could see and crystal-clear streams meandered through the landscape.

He turned to Jack, his eyes shining with gratitude. "Thank you," he said, his voice barely above a whisper.

Jack merely nodded, his eyes twinkling with mischief. "Remember, young lad, the greatest adventures are often found in the most unexpected places."

And with that, Jack disappeared into the ether, leaving Tommy alone to explore this newfound paradise.

As he wandered through the enchanted forest, Tommy couldn't help but marvel at the wonders of the world. For in that moment, he realized that life was indeed a grand adventure, full of mystery and magic just waiting to be discovered.

And so, with a smile on his face and a heart full of wonder, Tommy set off into the unknown, eager to uncover the secrets that lay hidden within The Enigma Tower.

Der rätselhafte Aufzug

IM HERZEN DES GESCHÄFTIGEN New York City, mitten zwischen den hoch aufragenden Wolkenkratzern, die die Wolken kratzen, stand ein eigenartiges Gebäude namens "Der Enigma-Turm". Es war eine Struktur, die schien, die Gesetze der architektonischen Logik zu trotzen, seine elegante Fassade geschmückt mit geheimnisvollen Symbolen, die in Gold graviert waren. Doch es war nicht die äußere Erscheinung, die die Stadtbewohner faszinierte; es war das, was verborgen lag - der rätselhafte Aufzug.

Nun, dieser Aufzug war keine gewöhnliche Vorrichtung. Es wurde gesagt, dass er über mystische Kräfte verfügte, die in der Lage waren, seine Passagiere nicht nur zwischen den Stockwerken, sondern durch Zeit und Raum selbst zu transportieren. Viele Geschichten kursierten über die seltsamen Vorkommnisse in seinen metallischen Begrenzungen, Flüstern von Personen, die eintraten und für immer verändert wieder herauskamen.

An einem tristen Dienstagnachmittag stand ein junger Junge namens Tommy vor dem Eingang zum Enigma-Turm. Er hatte die Gerüchte gehört, die verlockenden Geschichten von Abenteuer und Geheimnis, die auf diejenigen warteten, die mutig genug waren, einzutreten. Mit einem Herzen voller

Neugier und einem Geist voller Staunen drückte Tommy die prunkvollen Türen auf und trat in die Lobby ein.

Das Innere war ebenso grandios wie die äußere Erscheinung, mit Marmorböden, die unter dem sanften Glanz von Kronleuchtern glänzten. Tommy näherte sich dem Aufzug vorsichtig, seine Augen weit vor Erwartung. Als er sich ausstreckte, um den Rufknopf zu drücken, sprach eine Stimme hinter ihm.

"Suchst du ein bisschen Aufregung, junger Bursche?"

Tommy drehte sich um und sah einen alten Mann, der in einem zerfetzten Mantel gekleidet war und ein schelmisches Grinsen trug.

"Wer bist du?" fragte Tommy, seine Stimme vor Aufregung zitternd.

Der alte Mann lachte. "Manche nennen mich den Hüter der Geheimnisse, andere kennen mich einfach als Jack. Aber genug von mir, bist du bereit, eine Reise anzutreten wie keine andere?"

Tommy nickte begeistert, sein Herz schlug ihm bis zum Hals. Ohne ein weiteres Wort deutete Jack auf den Aufzug, und Tommy trat ein, die Türen schlossen sich hinter ihm mit einem leisen Zischen.

Als der Aufzug zu steigen begann, spürte Tommy eine merkwürdige Empfindung über sich kommen, wie ein Wirbelwind von Emotionen, der in seinem Kopf wirbelte. Die Wände des Aufzugs schienen zu schimmern und sich zu verformen, sich in Szenen aus einer fernen Vergangenheit zu verwandeln.

Er fand sich auf den geschäftigen Straßen von New York der 1920er Jahre wieder, umgeben von Flappern und Gangstern. Die Luft war schwer von den Klängen des Jazz und dem Duft von illegalen Bars der Prohibitionszeit. Tommy staunte, als sich die Stadt vor seinen Augen in ein Kaleidoskop von Farben und Kulturen verwandelte.

Aber genauso schnell, wie es begonnen hatte, verschob sich die Szene erneut. Jetzt fand sich Tommy in einer futuristischen Metropole wieder, in der Flugautos durch die Luft sausten und Roboter die Straßen bevölkerten. Er staunte über die technologischen Wunder, die ihn umgaben, seine Augen weit vor Staunen.

Mit jedem Stockwerk, das sie passierten, wuchs Tommys Staunen, sein Durst nach Abenteuer unstillbar. Es war, als ob der Enigma-Turm zu einem Portal zu tausend verschiedenen Welten geworden war, jede fantastischer als die andere.

Schließlich, nachdem sich der Aufzug wie eine Ewigkeit angefühlt hatte, hielt er an, und die Türen öffneten sich, um einen Anblick zu enthüllen wie keinen anderen. Tommy trat in ein üppiges Paradies, wo smaragdgrüne Wälder sich bis zum Horizont erstreckten und kristallklare Bäche durch die Landschaft mäanderten.

Er wandte sich an Jack, seine Augen glänzten vor Dankbarkeit. "Danke", sagte er, seine Stimme kaum über ein Flüstern.

Jack nickte nur, seine Augen funkelten vor Schalk. "Denk daran, junger Bursche, die größten Abenteuer werden oft an den unerwartetsten Orten gefunden."

Und damit verschwand Jack in der Äther, ließ Tommy allein, um dieses neu gefundene Paradies zu erkunden.

Als er durch den verzauberten Wald wanderte, konnte Tommy nicht anders, als über die Wunder der Welt zu staunen. Denn in diesem Moment erkannte er, dass das Leben in der Tat ein großes Abenteuer war, voller Geheimnisse und Magie, die darauf warteten, entdeckt zu werden.

Und so, mit einem Lächeln im Gesicht und einem Herzen voller Staunen, machte sich Tommy auf ins Unbekannte, begierig darauf, die Geheimnisse zu enthüllen, die im Enigma-Turm verborgen lagen.

Neon Nights

IN THE HEART OF NEW York City, where the streets hummed with the rhythm of life and the neon lights danced like fireflies in the night sky, there existed a world within a world—a realm where dreams collided with reality and the boundaries between them blurred like the edges of a jazz riff. This was the domain of the nocturnal wanderers, the restless souls who roamed the city streets in search of something more, something beyond the confines of ordinary existence.

Among these wanderers was a young man named Johnny, a poet with a penchant for the unconventional and a thirst for adventure that burned brighter than the lights of Times Square. He moved through the city like a shadow, his eyes wide with wonder and his mind ablaze with inspiration.

On a warm summer evening, Johnny found himself standing on the corner of 42nd Street and Broadway, the epicenter of New York's vibrant nightlife. The streets pulsed with energy, the air thick with the scent of excitement and possibility.

With a cigarette dangling from his lips and a beat-up notebook tucked under his arm, Johnny set off into the neon-lit maze of the city, his footsteps echoing against the pavement like the rhythm of a distant drum.

He wandered through the labyrinthine streets of Greenwich Village, where bohemian artists and beatnik poets congregated in smoky coffeehouses, their voices rising and falling in a symphony of words and music. Johnny listened intently, absorbing the stories and experiences of those around him like a sponge, his mind spinning with ideas and imagery.

As the night wore on, Johnny found himself drawn to the pulsating heartbeat of the city—the jazz clubs that lined the streets of Harlem like jewels in a crown. He pushed open the door of a dimly lit club, the sound of saxophones and trumpets washing over him like a tidal wave.

Inside, the air was thick with smoke and the scent of bourbon, the music weaving its way through the crowd like a hypnotic spell. Johnny found a table in the corner and settled in, his eyes fixed on the stage where a band of musicians played with a fervor that bordered on madness.

He lost himself in the music, his body swaying to the rhythm like a leaf caught in a whirlwind. The hours slipped away like grains of sand through an hourglass, the world outside fading into oblivion as Johnny became one with the music, his soul soaring on the wings of improvisation.

As the first light of dawn began to creep over the horizon, Johnny emerged from the jazz club, his mind buzzing with inspiration and his heart full of longing. He wandered the deserted streets of the city, his footsteps echoing in the pre-dawn stillness.

And then, as if by some twist of fate, he found himself standing on the edge of Central Park, the sky ablaze with the colors of sunrise. He climbed to the top of a hill and sat down, his eyes fixed on the endless expanse of the city spread out before him like a vast ocean.

In that moment, Johnny felt a sense of peace wash over him, a feeling of belonging that he had never experienced before. For he realized that in the chaos and cacophony of the city, he had found his true home—a place where he could be free to roam and explore, to dream and create, to live life on his own terms.

And so, as the first rays of sunlight broke through the clouds, Johnny closed his eyes and let the warmth wash over him, his heart filled with gratitude for the city that had given him everything he had ever wanted and more.

For in the city that never sleeps, amidst the neon lights and the endless possibilities, Johnny had found his purpose—to live each moment as if it were his last, to embrace the beauty and the madness of life with open arms, and to never stop wandering, never stop dreaming, never stop searching for that elusive spark of inspiration that would ignite the flames of his soul and set him free.

Neon-Nächte

IM HERZEN VON NEW YORK City, wo die Straßen mit dem Rhythmus des Lebens summten und die Neonlichter wie Glühwürmchen am Nachthimmel tanzten, existierte eine Welt innerhalb einer Welt - ein Reich, in dem Träume mit der Realität kollidierten und die Grenzen zwischen ihnen verschwammen wie die Kanten einer Jazzmelodie. Dies war das Reich der nächtlichen Wanderer, der ruhelosen Seelen, die die Straßen der Stadt durchstreiften auf der Suche nach etwas Mehr, etwas Jenseits der Grenzen des gewöhnlichen Daseins.

Unter diesen Wanderern war ein junger Mann namens Johnny, ein Dichter mit einer Vorliebe für das Ungewöhnliche und einem Durst nach Abenteuer, der heller brannte als die Lichter des Times Square. Er bewegte sich wie ein Schatten durch die Stadt, seine Augen weit vor Staunen und sein Geist in Flammen der Inspiration.

An einem warmen Sommerabend fand sich Johnny auf der Ecke der 42nd Street und Broadway wieder, dem Epizentrum des lebendigen Nachtlebens von New York. Die Straßen pulsierten vor Energie, die Luft war dick vom Duft der Aufregung und der Möglichkeit.

Mit einer Zigarette im Mundwinkel und einem abgenutzten Notizbuch unter dem Arm machte sich Johnny auf in das neonbeleuchtete Labyrinth der Stadt, seine Schritte hallten gegen das Pflaster wie der Rhythmus eines entfernten Trommels.

Er wanderte durch die labyrinthartigen Straßen von Greenwich Village, wo bohemische Künstler und Beatnik-Dichter sich in rauchigen Kaffeehäusern versammelten, ihre Stimmen in einer Symphonie aus Worten und Musik auf- und abschwellend. Johnny hörte aufmerksam zu, sog die Geschichten und Erfahrungen der Menschen um sich herum auf wie ein Schwamm, sein Geist wirbelte vor Ideen und Bildern.

Als die Nacht voranschritt, fühlte sich Johnny von dem pulsierenden Herzschlag der Stadt angezogen - den Jazzclubs, die die Straßen von Harlem wie Juwelen in einer Krone säumten. Er drückte die Tür eines spärlich beleuchteten Clubs auf, der Klang von Saxophonen und Trompeten überflutete ihn wie eine Flutwelle.

Im Inneren lag Rauch in der Luft und der Duft von Bourbon, die Musik schlängelte sich wie ein hypnotischer Zauber durch die Menge. Johnny fand einen Tisch in der Ecke und ließ sich nieder, seine Augen auf die Bühne gerichtet, wo eine Band von Musikern mit einer Leidenschaft spielte, die an Wahnsinn grenzte.

Er verlor sich in der Musik, sein Körper wiegte sich im Rhythmus wie ein Blatt im Wirbelwind. Die Stunden vergingen wie Sandkörner in einer Sanduhr, die Welt draußen verschwand in der Vergessenheit, als Johnny eins wurde mit der Musik, seine Seele erhob sich auf den Flügeln der Improvisation.

Als das erste Licht der Morgendämmerung über den Horizont kroch, verließ Johnny den Jazzclub, sein Geist summte vor Inspiration und sein Herz war voller Sehnsucht. Er wanderte durch die verlassenen Straßen der Stadt, seine Schritte hallten in der Stille vor der Morgendämmerung wider.

Und dann, als wäre es von einem Schicksalsschlag, fand er sich am Rand des Central Parks stehend, der Himmel leuchtete in den Farben des Sonnenaufgangs. Er stieg auf einen Hügel und setzte sich, seine Augen auf die endlose Weite der Stadt gerichtet, die sich vor ihm ausbreitete wie ein weites Meer.

In diesem Moment spürte Johnny eine tiefe Ruhe über sich kommen, ein Gefühl des Zugehörigseins, das er noch nie zuvor erlebt hatte. Denn er erkannte, dass er inmitten des Chaos und der Kakophonie der Stadt sein wahres Zuhause gefunden hatte - einen Ort, an dem er frei sein konnte, zu wandern und zu erkunden, zu träumen und zu schaffen, das Leben nach seinen eigenen Vorstellungen zu leben.

Und so, als die ersten Sonnenstrahlen durch die Wolken brachen, schloss Johnny die Augen und ließ die Wärme über sich hinwegspülen, sein Herz erfüllt von Dankbarkeit für die Stadt, die ihm alles gegeben hatte, was er je wollte und mehr.

Denn in der Stadt, die niemals schläft, inmitten der Neonlichter und der endlosen Möglichkeiten, hatte Johnny seinen Zweck gefunden - jeden Moment zu leben, als wäre es sein letzter, die Schönheit und den Wahnsinn des Lebens mit offenen Armen zu umarmen und niemals aufzuhören zu wandern, niemals aufzuhören zu träumen, niemals aufzuhören zu suchen nach diesem flüchtigen Funken der Inspiration, der die Flammen seiner Seele entzünden und ihn frei setzen würde.

Tales of Manhattan

IN THE HEART OF NEW York City, where the streets teemed with life and the skyscrapers reached for the heavens, there existed a world of magic and mystery hidden beneath the surface—a world where the ordinary intertwined with the extraordinary, and the lines between reality and fantasy blurred like watercolors in the rain. This was the realm of the storytellers, the weavers of tales who spun their narratives from the threads of everyday life, transforming the mundane into the miraculous with the flick of a pen.

Among these storytellers was a woman named Sofia, a writer with a passion for the enigmatic and a penchant for the supernatural. She moved through the city like a ghost, her eyes sharp and her mind alight with curiosity, always searching for the next great story to unfold before her.

On a brisk autumn evening, Sofia found herself wandering the streets of Greenwich Village, where the air was thick with the scent of spices and the sound of laughter echoed off the cobblestone streets. She wandered into a cozy cafe tucked away in a quiet corner, the aroma of freshly brewed coffee drawing her in like a moth to a flame.

As she settled into a corner booth, Sofia watched the world go by outside the window, her mind drifting like smoke on the wind. She sipped her coffee slowly, savoring the rich flavors as she pondered the mysteries of the universe.

Suddenly, a voice broke through the haze of her thoughts—a voice belonging to a man seated at the table next to hers. He was an elderly gentleman with twinkling eyes and a mischievous grin, his face weathered with age but his spirit as vibrant as ever.

"Excuse me, miss," he said, his voice tinged with a hint of intrigue. "I couldn't help but notice your notebook. Are you a writer?"

Sofia nodded, her curiosity piqued. "Yes, I am. And you?"

The man chuckled, his eyes sparkling with amusement. "Some call me the Keeper of Secrets, others simply know me as Leo. But enough about me, tell me, what tales do you have hidden within those pages?"

And so, Sofia began to weave her stories, her words flowing like rivers of ink as she spoke of love and loss, of triumph and tragedy, of the countless lives that intersected and intertwined in the bustling metropolis of New York City. She spoke of a young couple who fell in love beneath the shadow of the Empire State Building, their romance doomed from the start but no less passionate for it. She spoke of a struggling artist who found inspiration in the most unlikely of places—a graffiti-covered alleyway in the heart of the Bronx. She spoke of a mysterious stranger who wandered the streets at night, his footsteps echoing like whispers in the darkness.

As Sofia spoke, Leo listened intently, his eyes shining with wonder and his heart full of longing. For he knew that within the labyrinthine tales of Manhattan lay the key to unlocking the secrets of the universe, the answers to questions that had plagued mankind since the dawn of time.

And so, as the night wore on and the cafe grew quiet, Sofia and Leo continued to share their stories, their voices blending together in a symphony of words and emotions. And in that moment, they knew that they had stumbled upon something truly magical—a connection that transcended time and space, a bond forged in the fires of creativity and fueled by the limitless power of the human imagination.

As the first light of dawn began to creep over the horizon, Sofia and Leo emerged from the cafe, their hearts light and their minds buzzing with inspiration. They walked through the empty streets of Greenwich Village, their footsteps echoing in the pre-dawn stillness.

And as they walked, Sofia felt a sense of peace wash over her, a feeling of belonging that she had never experienced before. For she realized that in the labyrinthine tales of Manhattan, she had found her true home—a place where she could be free to explore and create, to dream and imagine, to weave her stories into the fabric of the city itself.

And so, hand in hand with Leo by her side, Sofia set off into the dawn, her heart full of hope and her spirit soaring on the wings of imagination. For in the city that never sleeps, amidst the towering skyscrapers and bustling streets, anything was possible—and the greatest adventure of all was yet to come.

Geschichten aus Manhattan

IM HERZEN VON NEW YORK City, wo die Straßen vor Leben pulsierten und die Wolkenkratzer in den Himmel ragten, existierte eine Welt aus Magie und Geheimnis, die unter der Oberfläche verborgen lag - eine Welt, in der das Gewöhnliche mit dem Außergewöhnlichen verwoben war und die Grenzen zwischen Realität und Fantasie sich wie Wasserfarben im Regen verschwammen. Dies war das Reich der Geschichtenerzähler, der Weber von Geschichten, die ihre Erzählungen aus den Fäden des täglichen Lebens spannen, das Alltägliche mit einem Federstrich in das Wunderbare verwandelten.

Unter diesen Geschichtenerzählern war eine Frau namens Sofia, eine Schriftstellerin mit einer Leidenschaft für das Rätselhafte und einem Hang zum Übernatürlichen. Sie bewegte sich wie ein Geist durch die Stadt, ihre Augen scharf und ihr Geist von Neugierde entfacht, immer auf der Suche nach der nächsten großartigen Geschichte, die sich vor ihr entfalten würde.

An einem kühlen Herbstabend fand sich Sofia auf den Straßen von Greenwich Village wieder, wo die Luft schwer war vom Duft der Gewürze und das Lachen von den Kopfsteinpflasterstraßen widerhallte. Sie schlenderte in ein gemütliches Café, das in einer ruhigen Ecke versteckt war, der Duft von frisch gebrühtem Kaffee zog sie an wie eine Motte zur Flamme.

Als sie sich in eine Ecke setzte, beobachtete Sofia das Treiben draußen durch das Fenster, ihr Geist trieb wie Rauch im Wind. Sie nippte langsam an ihrem Kaffee, die reichen Aromen genießend, während sie über die Geheimnisse des Universums nachdachte.

Plötzlich durchbrach eine Stimme den Dunst ihrer Gedanken - eine Stimme, die einem Mann gehörte, der an dem Tisch neben ihr saß. Er war ein älterer Herr mit funkelnden Augen und einem verschmitzten Grinsen, sein Gesicht vom Alter gezeichnet, aber sein Geist so lebendig wie eh und je.

"Entschuldigen Sie, Fräulein", sagte er, seine Stimme von einem Hauch von Neugierde geprägt. "Ich konnte nicht umhin, Ihr Notizbuch zu bemerken. Sind Sie eine Schriftstellerin?"

Sofia nickte, ihre Neugier geweckt. "Ja, das bin ich. Und Sie?"

Der Mann lachte, seine Augen funkelten vor Amüsement. "Manche nennen mich den Hüter der Geheimnisse, andere kennen mich einfach als Leo. Aber genug von mir, erzählen Sie mir, welche Geschichten haben Sie in diesen Seiten verborgen?"

Und so begann Sofia, ihre Geschichten zu weben, ihre Worte flossen wie Flüsse von Tinte, während sie von Liebe und Verlust sprach, von Triumph und Tragödie, von den unzähligen Leben, die sich in der geschäftigen Metropole New York City kreuzten und verflochten. Sie erzählte von einem jungen Paar, das sich im Schatten des Empire State Building verliebte, ihre Romanze von Anfang an zum Scheitern verurteilt, aber nicht weniger leidenschaftlich deshalb. Sie sprach von einem kämpfenden Künstler, der Inspiration an den ungewöhnlichsten Orten fand

- einer mit Graffiti übersäten Gasse im Herzen der Bronx. Sie sprach von einem geheimnisvollen Fremden, der nachts durch die Straßen wanderte, seine Schritte wie Flüstern in der Dunkelheit.

Während Sofia sprach, hörte Leo aufmerksam zu, seine Augen leuchteten vor Staunen und sein Herz war voller Sehnsucht. Denn er wusste, dass in den labyrinthartigen Geschichten von Manhattan der Schlüssel lag, um die Geheimnisse des Universums zu entschlüsseln, die Antworten auf Fragen, die die Menschheit seit Anbeginn der Zeit geplagt hatten.

Und so, während die Nacht verging und das Café still wurde, teilten Sofia und Leo weiterhin ihre Geschichten, ihre Stimmen verschmolzen zu einer Symphonie aus Worten und Emotionen. Und in diesem Moment wussten sie, dass sie auf etwas wirklich Magisches gestoßen waren - eine Verbindung, die Raum und Zeit überdauerte, eine Bindung, die in den Feuern der Kreativität geschmiedet und von der grenzenlosen Kraft der menschlichen Vorstellungskraft genährt wurde.

Als das erste Licht der Morgendämmerung über den Horizont kroch, verließen Sofia und Leo das Café, ihre Herzen leicht und ihre Köpfe voller Inspiration. Sie schlenderten durch die leeren Straßen von Greenwich Village, ihre Schritte hallten in der Morgendämmerungsstille wider.

Und während sie gingen, spürte Sofia eine tiefe Ruhe über sich kommen, ein Gefühl des Zugehörigseins, das sie noch nie zuvor erlebt hatte. Denn sie erkannte, dass sie in den labyrinthartigen Geschichten von Manhattan ihr wahres Zuhause gefunden hatte

- einen Ort, an dem sie frei sein konnte, zu erkunden und zu erschaffen, zu träumen und sich vorzustellen, ihre Geschichten in den Stoff der Stadt selbst zu weben.

Und so, Hand in Hand mit Leo an ihrer Seite, machte sich Sofia in die Morgendämmerung auf, ihr Herz voller Hoffnung und ihr Geist auf den Flügeln der Vorstellungskraft schwebend. Denn in der Stadt, die niemals schläft, zwischen den hoch aufragenden Wolkenkratzern und den belebten Straßen, war alles möglich - und das größte Abenteuer aller Zeiten stand noch bevor.

Love in the Big Apple

IN THE BUSTLING METROPOLIS of New York City, where the streets buzzed with life and the skyline sparkled like a jeweled crown, there existed a world of romance and whimsy hidden behind every corner—a world where love bloomed like wildflowers in a concrete jungle, and the air crackled with the electricity of possibility. This was the realm of the hopeless romantics, the dreamers who believed in happy endings and fairy tale love stories, even in a city as chaotic and unpredictable as New York.

Among these romantics was a young woman named Lily, a wide-eyed optimist with a penchant for the fantastical and a heart as big as the city itself. She moved through the streets with a spring in her step and a smile on her lips, her eyes sparkling with the promise of adventure.

On a crisp spring morning, Lily found herself standing in line at her favorite bakery, the aroma of freshly baked croissants wafting through the air like a siren's song. She watched eagerly as the baker behind the counter expertly crafted each pastry with practiced hands, his movements as graceful as a ballet dancer's.

As she reached the front of the line, Lily placed her order with a smile, her heart fluttering with anticipation. But just as the baker was about to hand her the bag of pastries, a commotion broke out at the door—a handsome stranger had stumbled in, his arms laden with books and papers, his face flushed with embarrassment.

"I'm so sorry!" he exclaimed, his cheeks turning crimson as he fumbled to gather his belongings. "I didn't mean to interrupt—"

But before he could finish his sentence, Lily stepped forward with a grin, her eyes alight with mischief.

"No need to apologize," she said, her voice soft but confident. "You can make it up to me by buying me a cup of coffee."

The stranger blinked in surprise, his gaze meeting Lily's with a mixture of confusion and intrigue.

"Um, sure," he stammered, his cheeks flushing even darker. "I mean, yes, of course. Coffee sounds great."

And so, with a laugh and a smile, Lily and the stranger set off into the city, their footsteps echoing against the pavement like a symphony of possibility. They wandered through the bustling streets of Manhattan, their conversation flowing effortlessly as they exchanged stories and laughter.

As they walked, Lily learned that the stranger's name was David, and that he was a writer with a passion for the written word and a love for the city that burned brighter than the sun. She listened intently as he spoke of his dreams and aspirations, his voice soft but filled with conviction.

And in turn, David learned that Lily was an artist with a flair for the dramatic and a heart as wild as the wind. He watched with fascination as she spoke of her latest project—a series of paintings inspired by the streets of New York, each one a masterpiece in its own right.

As the day wore on and the sun began to sink beneath the horizon, Lily and David found themselves standing on the banks of the Hudson River, the lights of the city twinkling in the distance like a million stars in the night sky. They sat down on a bench overlooking the water, their hands brushing against each other like the gentlest of whispers.

And in that moment, as the world around them faded into darkness and the sounds of the city fell away to nothing, Lily and David knew that they had stumbled upon something truly magical—a connection that transcended time and space, a bond forged in the fires of passion and fueled by the limitless power of love.

And so, hand in hand beneath the twinkling lights of the city, Lily and David set off into the night, their hearts full and their souls intertwined in a dance as old as time itself. For in the city that never sleeps, amidst the chaos and confusion of everyday life, they had found something truly extraordinary—a love that would withstand the test of time and endure forever in the hearts of two kindred spirits, united in their shared journey through the streets of New York.

Liebe im Big Apple

IN DER GESCHÄFTIGEN Metropole New York City, wo die Straßen vor Leben pulsierten und die Skyline wie eine juwelenbesetzte Krone funkelte, existierte eine Welt der Romantik und Launenhaftigkeit, die hinter jeder Ecke verborgen lag - eine Welt, in der die Liebe wie Wildblumen in einem Beton-Dschungel blühte und die Luft von der Elektrizität der Möglichkeiten knisterte. Dies war das Reich der hoffnungslosen Romantiker, der Träumer, die an Happy Ends und Märchenliebesgeschichten glaubten, selbst in einer Stadt so chaotisch und unberechenbar wie New York.

Unter diesen Romantikern war eine junge Frau namens Lily, eine optimistische Träumerin mit einer Vorliebe für das Fantastische und einem Herzen so groß wie die Stadt selbst. Sie bewegte sich mit einem Sprung in ihrem Schritt und einem Lächeln auf den Lippen durch die Straßen, ihre Augen glitzernd vor Abenteuerlust.

An einem klaren Frühlingsmorgen fand sich Lily in der Schlange vor ihrer Lieblingsbäckerei wieder, der Duft von frisch gebackenen Croissants zog durch die Luft wie der Gesang einer Sirene. Sie beobachtete gespannt, wie der Bäcker hinter dem Tresen jeden Keks mit geübten Händen kunstvoll herstellte, seine Bewegungen so graziös wie die eines Balletttänzers.

Als sie an die Reihe kam, gab Lily lächelnd ihre Bestellung auf, ihr Herz flatterte vor Vorfreude. Doch gerade als der Bäcker ihr die Tüte mit Gebäck geben wollte, brach draußen an der Tür ein Tumult aus - ein gutaussehender Fremder war hereingestolpert, seine Arme beladen mit Büchern und Papieren, sein Gesicht vor Verlegenheit gerötet.

"Es tut mir so leid!" rief er aus, seine Wangen vor Verlegenheit errötend, während er versuchte, seine Sachen zusammenzuraffen. "Ich wollte nicht stören -"

Aber bevor er seinen Satz beenden konnte, trat Lily mit einem Grinsen vor, ihre Augen leuchtend vor Schalkhaftigkeit.

"Entschuldigung ist nicht nötig", sagte sie, ihre Stimme leise, aber selbstbewusst. "Du kannst es mir wiedergutmachen, indem du mir einen Kaffee kaufst."

Der Fremde blinzelte überrascht, sein Blick traf den von Lily mit einer Mischung aus Verwirrung und Neugier.

"Ähm, sicher", stammelte er, seine Wangen noch dunkler errötend. "Ich meine, ja, natürlich. Kaffee klingt gut."

Und so, mit einem Lachen und einem Lächeln, machten sich Lily und der Fremde auf den Weg durch die Stadt, ihre Schritte hallten gegen das Pflaster wie eine Symphonie der Möglichkeiten. Sie wanderten durch die belebten Straßen von Manhattan, ihre Unterhaltung floss mühelos, während sie Geschichten und Gelächter austauschten.

Während sie gingen, erfuhr Lily, dass der Fremde David hieß und dass er ein Schriftsteller mit einer Leidenschaft für das geschriebene Wort war und eine Liebe für die Stadt hatte, die heller als die Sonne brannte. Sie hörte aufmerksam zu, als er von seinen Träumen und Hoffnungen sprach, seine Stimme leise, aber voller Überzeugung.

Und im Gegenzug erfuhr David, dass Lily eine Künstlerin mit einem Hang zum Dramatischen und einem Herzen so wild wie der Wind war. Fasziniert beobachtete er, wie sie von ihrem neuesten Projekt sprach - einer Serie von Gemälden, inspiriert von den Straßen New Yorks, von denen jedes ein Meisterwerk für sich war.

Als der Tag verging und die Sonne begann, hinter dem Horizont zu versinken, fanden sich Lily und David am Ufer des Hudson River wieder, die Lichter der Stadt glitzerten in der Ferne wie Millionen Sterne am Nachthimmel. Sie setzten sich auf eine Bank mit Blick auf das Wasser, ihre Hände berührten sich wie das sanfteste Flüstern.

Und in diesem Moment, als die Welt um sie herum in Dunkelheit versank und die Geräusche der Stadt verstummten, wussten Lily und David, dass sie auf etwas wirklich Magisches gestoßen waren - eine Verbindung, die Raum und Zeit überdauerte, eine Bindung, die in den Feuern der Leidenschaft geschmiedet wurde und von der grenzenlosen Kraft der Liebe genährt wurde.

Und so machten sich Lily und David Hand in Hand unter den glitzernden Lichtern der Stadt in die Nacht auf, ihre Herzen voll und ihre Seelen in einem Tanz verschlungen, so alt wie die Zeit selbst. Denn in der Stadt, die niemals schläft, inmitten des

Chaos und der Verwirrung des täglichen Lebens, hatten sie etwas wirklich Außergewöhnliches gefunden - eine Liebe, die den Test der Zeit bestehen und für immer in den Herzen zweier verwandter Seelen bestehen würde, vereint in ihrer gemeinsamen Reise durch die Straßen von New York.

Shadows of the City

IN THE LABYRINTHINE streets of New York City, where the shadows danced like specters in the night and the secrets of the city lay hidden beneath the surface, there existed a world of intrigue and danger lurking around every corner—a world where heroes and villains clashed in a never-ending battle for supremacy, and the line between right and wrong blurred like the edges of a foggy mirror. This was the realm of the clandestine operatives, the agents of deception who moved through the shadows with the grace of predators stalking their prey, their every move calculated and precise.

Among these operatives was a man named Jack, a former intelligence agent with a dark past and a penchant for the dangerous. He moved through the city like a ghost, his presence known only to those who dared to cross him, his eyes sharp and his mind sharper still.

On a cold winter's night, Jack found himself standing on the rooftop of a skyscraper overlooking the glittering expanse of Manhattan, the lights of the city shimmering like diamonds in the darkness. He peered through the scope of his rifle, his gaze fixed on his target—a notorious crime boss known only as The Snake.

For weeks, Jack had been tracking The Snake's movements, gathering evidence of his illicit activities and building a case against him. And now, as the city slept below him, Jack knew that the time had come to take action—to rid the streets of New York of this dangerous threat once and for all.

With a steady hand and a steady aim, Jack squeezed the trigger, the gunshot echoing through the night like thunder. The bullet found its mark, striking The Snake in the chest and sending him tumbling to the ground below. And as Jack watched from his perch high above the city, he felt a sense of satisfaction wash over him—a job well done, another victory for justice in the never-ending war against crime.

But just as Jack was about to make his escape, a voice spoke from behind him—a voice filled with menace and malice.

"Nice shot, Jack," it said, its tone dripping with sarcasm. "But you should know better than to mess with me."

Jack turned to see a figure emerging from the shadows—a man cloaked in darkness, his face obscured by a mask.

"Who are you?" Jack demanded, his hand reaching for his gun.

The figure chuckled, a cold, humorless sound that sent shivers down Jack's spine.

"You can call me The Phantom," he said, his voice like ice. "And I'm here to finish what The Snake started."

With lightning speed, The Phantom lunged at Jack, his fists flying like daggers in the night. Jack fought back with all his strength, his years of training kicking in as he countered each blow with precision and skill.

But The Phantom was relentless, his attacks fueled by rage and determination. He pressed on, his blows raining down on Jack like a hailstorm in the desert.

And then, just when it seemed that all hope was lost, Jack saw an opportunity—a glimmer of light in the darkness. With one final, desperate effort, he delivered a powerful blow to The Phantom's chest, sending him staggering backwards towards the edge of the rooftop.

And as The Phantom teetered on the brink of oblivion, Jack reached out with a steady hand and pulled him back from the edge, his eyes meeting The Phantom's with a mixture of defiance and determination.

"This ends here," Jack said, his voice steady despite the adrenaline coursing through his veins. "No more games, no more violence. It's time to put an end to this once and for all."

The Phantom stared at Jack with a mixture of shock and disbelief, his mask slipping from his face to reveal the features of a man worn and weary from years of fighting.

"You're right," he said, his voice barely above a whisper. "It's time to let go of the past and embrace the future. Together, we can make a difference in this city."

And so, with a handshake and a shared sense of purpose, Jack and The Phantom set off into the night, their footsteps echoing through the empty streets of New York like the beat of a drum.

For in the shadows of the city, amidst the chaos and confusion of everyday life, they had found something truly extraordinary—a bond forged in the fires of adversity and fueled by the limitless power of redemption. And as they walked side by side into the unknown, they knew that no matter what challenges lay ahead, they would face them together, united in their shared commitment to making the world a safer and more just place for all who called it home.

Schatten der Stadt

IN DEN LABYRINTHARTIGEN Straßen von New York City, wo die Schatten wie Gespenster in der Nacht tanzten und die Geheimnisse der Stadt unter der Oberfläche verborgen lagen, existierte eine Welt voller Intrigen und Gefahren, die an jeder Ecke lauerten - eine Welt, in der Helden und Schurken in einem nie endenden Kampf um die Vorherrschaft kämpften und die Grenze zwischen Gut und Böse sich wie die Ränder eines nebligen Spiegels verschwamm. Dies war das Reich der geheimen Agenten, der Agenten der Täuschung, die sich mit der Anmut von Raubtieren, die ihre Beute belauern, durch die Schatten bewegten, jede ihrer Bewegungen kalkuliert und präzise.

Unter diesen Agenten war ein Mann namens Jack, ein ehemaliger Geheimagent mit einer dunklen Vergangenheit und einer Vorliebe für das Gefährliche. Er bewegte sich wie ein Geist durch die Stadt, seine Anwesenheit nur denen bekannt, die es wagten, sich ihm zu widersetzen, seine Augen scharf und sein Verstand noch schärfer.

An einem kalten Winterabend fand sich Jack auf dem Dach eines Wolkenkratzers wieder, der über die glitzernde Weite von Manhattan hinwegblickte, die Lichter der Stadt schimmerten wie Diamanten in der Dunkelheit. Er spähte durch das Zielfernrohr seines Gewehrs, sein Blick auf sein Ziel gerichtet -

ein berüchtigter Verbrecher, der nur als Die Schlange bekannt war.

Wochenlang hatte Jack die Bewegungen von Die Schlange verfolgt, Beweise für seine illegalen Aktivitäten gesammelt und gegen ihn ermittelt. Und jetzt, als die Stadt unter ihm schlief, wusste Jack, dass die Zeit gekommen war, zu handeln - die Straßen von New York von dieser gefährlichen Bedrohung für immer zu befreien.

Mit einer ruhigen Hand und einem sicheren Ziel drückte Jack den Abzug, der Schuss hallte durch die Nacht wie Donner. Die Kugel traf ihr Ziel, traf Die Schlange in die Brust und schickte ihn taumelnd zu Boden. Und als Jack von seinem Aussichtspunkt hoch über der Stadt zusah, spürte er ein Gefühl der Befriedigung - eine gut gemachte Arbeit, ein weiterer Sieg für die Gerechtigkeit im nie endenden Kampf gegen das Verbrechen.

Aber gerade als Jack dabei war, seine Flucht anzutreten, erklang eine Stimme hinter ihm - eine Stimme voller Bedrohung und Bosheit.

"Guter Schuss, Jack", sagte sie, ihr Ton von Sarkasmus triefend. "Aber du solltest besser wissen, als dich mit mir anzulegen."

Jack drehte sich um und sah eine Gestalt aus den Schatten treten - einen Mann, der von Dunkelheit umhüllt war, sein Gesicht von einer Maske verdeckt.

"Wer bist du?" forderte Jack und griff nach seiner Waffe.

Die Gestalt lachte, ein kaltes, humorloses Geräusch, das Jack eine Gänsehaut verursachte.

"Du kannst mich den Phantom nennen", sagte er, seine Stimme wie Eis. "Und ich bin hier, um zu vollenden, was Die Schlange begonnen hat."

Mit blitzschneller Geschwindigkeit stürzte der Phantom auf Jack zu, seine Fäuste flogen wie Dolche in der Nacht. Jack wehrte sich mit aller Kraft, seine jahrelange Ausbildung setzte ein, als er jeden Schlag mit Präzision und Geschick abwehrte.

Aber der Phantom war unerbittlich, seine Angriffe wurden von Wut und Entschlossenheit angetrieben. Er drängte vorwärts, seine Schläge prasselten wie Hagel auf Jack herab.

Und dann, gerade als es schien, als sei alle Hoffnung verloren, sah Jack eine Gelegenheit - ein Schimmer Licht in der Dunkelheit. Mit einem letzten verzweifelten Anstrengung versetzte er dem Phantom einen kräftigen Schlag in die Brust, sodass es rückwärts an den Rand des Dachs taumelte.

Und als der Phantom am Abgrund der Vergessenheit wankte, griff Jack mit einer ruhigen Hand nach ihm und zog ihn zurück, seine Augen trafen die des Phantoms mit einer Mischung aus Trotz und Entschlossenheit.

"Das endet hier", sagte Jack, seine Stimme ruhig trotz des Adrenalins, das durch seine Adern raste. "Keine Spiele mehr, keine Gewalt mehr. Es ist Zeit, dem ein für alle Mal ein Ende zu setzen."

Der Phantom starrte Jack mit einer Mischung aus Schock und Unglauben an, seine Maske glitt von seinem Gesicht und enthüllte die Züge eines Mannes, der von Jahren des Kampfes abgekämpft war.

"Du hast recht", sagte er, seine Stimme kaum mehr als ein Flüstern. "Es ist Zeit, die Vergangenheit loszulassen und die Zukunft zu umarmen. Gemeinsam können wir einen Unterschied in dieser Stadt machen."

Und so machten sich Jack und der Phantom Hand in Hand in die Nacht auf, ihre Schritte hallten durch die leeren Straßen von New York wie der Schlag eines Trommels.

Denn in den Schatten der Stadt, mitten im Chaos und der Verwirrung des Alltags, hatten sie etwas wirklich Außergewöhnliches gefunden - eine Bindung, die in den Feuern der Widrigkeiten geschmiedet wurde und von der grenzenlosen Kraft der Erlösung genährt wurde. Und während sie nebeneinander in das Unbekannte gingen, wussten sie, dass ihnen egal waren, welche Herausforderungen noch bevorstanden, sie würden sie gemeinsam meistern, vereint in ihrem gemeinsamen Engagement, die Welt zu einem sichereren und gerechteren Ort für all jene zu machen, die sie ihr Zuhause nannten.

The Brownstone Chronicles

IN A CHARMING BROWNSTONE nestled amidst the bustling streets of New York City, where the sounds of traffic and the scent of hot pretzels wafted through the air, there existed a world of quiet charm and gentle intrigue—a world where the lives of ordinary people intersected in the most unexpected ways, and every corner held a story waiting to be told. This was the realm of the residents of 221B Maple Street, a diverse community bound together by the bonds of friendship and neighborly camaraderie.

Among these residents was a retired schoolteacher named Mrs. Thompson, a kindly widow with a penchant for gardening and a love for her beloved cat, Mr. Jeremy. She lived alone in her cozy apartment on the second floor, her days spent tending to her plants and baking batches of her famous chocolate chip cookies to share with her neighbors.

On a bright spring morning, Mrs. Thompson found herself in the midst of her daily routine, watering her plants and humming a tune to herself as she worked. Suddenly, there was a knock at the door—a soft, hesitant rap that echoed through the hallway like the fluttering of a butterfly's wings.

Curious, Mrs. Thompson hurried to answer the door, her heart pounding with anticipation. To her surprise, she found her neighbor, Mr. Patel, standing on the doorstep, his face creased with worry.

"Mrs. Thompson, I need your help," he said, his voice trembling with emotion. "My daughter, she's gone missing. I don't know what to do."

Mrs. Thompson's heart went out to Mr. Patel, her maternal instincts kicking into high gear. Without hesitation, she invited him inside and offered him a seat at her kitchen table, a comforting presence in the midst of his turmoil.

Together, they sat and talked, Mrs. Thompson lending a sympathetic ear as Mr. Patel poured out his fears and frustrations. And as they spoke, Mrs. Thompson couldn't help but feel a sense of determination welling up inside her—a desire to help her neighbor in any way she could.

And so, with a steely resolve and a twinkle in her eye, Mrs. Thompson set off into the city, her mind buzzing with possibilities. She visited the local police station, where she spoke to the officers and provided them with all the information she could gather about Mr. Patel's missing daughter. She distributed flyers and spoke to neighbors, rallying the community together in a show of solidarity and support.

And as the days turned into weeks and the search for Mr. Patel's daughter stretched on, Mrs. Thompson refused to give up hope. She spent her days and nights scouring the city, following every lead and leaving no stone unturned in her quest to bring the missing girl home.

And then, just when it seemed that all hope was lost, Mrs. Thompson received a phone call—a call that would change everything. It was from a young woman who claimed to have seen Mr. Patel's daughter wandering the streets of Manhattan, her face pale and her eyes filled with fear.

With a sense of urgency, Mrs. Thompson set off into the night, her heart pounding in her chest as she raced through the streets of the city. And then, just as she was about to give up, she spotted a figure huddled in the doorway of an abandoned building—a figure that looked remarkably like Mr. Patel's daughter.

With a cry of joy, Mrs. Thompson rushed forward, her arms outstretched as she enveloped the young girl in a warm embrace. And as they stood there in the glow of the streetlights, Mrs. Thompson felt a sense of relief wash over her—a sense of fulfillment that came from knowing that she had made a difference in someone's life.

And so, with Mr. Patel's daughter safe in her arms, Mrs. Thompson led her back to the brownstone on Maple Street, where the community had gathered to welcome her home with open arms. And as they celebrated into the night, sharing stories and laughter in the warm embrace of friendship and neighborly love, Mrs. Thompson couldn't help but feel a sense of pride in her small corner of the world—a corner filled with the kind of kindness and compassion that made New York City feel like home.

Die Geschichten vom Brownstone

IN EINEM CHARMANTEN Brownstone, eingebettet in den belebten Straßen von New York City, wo der Klang des Verkehrs und der Duft von warmen Brezeln durch die Luft wehten, existierte eine Welt von ruhigem Charme und sanfter Intrige - eine Welt, in der sich das Leben gewöhnlicher Menschen auf unerwartete Weise kreuzte und an jeder Ecke eine Geschichte wartete, erzählt zu werden. Dies war das Reich der Bewohner von 221B Maple Street, einer vielfältigen Gemeinschaft, die durch die Bande der Freundschaft und nachbarschaftlichen Kameradschaft verbunden war.

Unter diesen Bewohnern war eine pensionierte Lehrerin namens Frau Thompson, eine freundliche Witwe mit einer Vorliebe für Gartenarbeit und einer Liebe zu ihrer geliebten Katze, Herrn Jeremy. Sie lebte allein in ihrer gemütlichen Wohnung im zweiten Stock, ihre Tage verbrachte sie damit, sich um ihre Pflanzen zu kümmern und Chargen ihrer berühmten Schokoladenkekse zu backen, um sie mit ihren Nachbarn zu teilen.

An einem strahlenden Frühlingsmorgen fand sich Frau Thompson mitten in ihrer täglichen Routine wieder, sie goss ihre Pflanzen und summte eine Melodie vor sich hin, während sie arbeitete. Plötzlich klopfte es an der Tür - ein leises, zögerndes

Klopfen, das durch den Flur hallte wie das Flattern der Flügel eines Schmetterlings.

Neugierig eilte Frau Thompson, um die Tür zu öffnen, ihr Herz klopfte vor Aufregung. Zu ihrer Überraschung fand sie ihren Nachbarn, Herrn Patel, vor ihrer Tür stehen, sein Gesicht von Sorge gezeichnet.

"Frau Thompson, ich brauche Ihre Hilfe", sagte er, seine Stimme zitterte vor Emotion. "Meine Tochter ist verschwunden. Ich weiß nicht, was ich tun soll."

Frau Thompsons Herz ging an Herrn Patel, ihre mütterlichen Instinkte wurden aktiviert. Ohne zu zögern, lud sie ihn ein und bot ihm einen Platz an ihrem Küchentisch an, eine tröstliche Präsenz inmitten seiner Wirren.

Gemeinsam saßen sie da und sprachen, Frau Thompson lieh ihm ein mitfühlendes Ohr, während Herr Patel seine Ängste und Frustrationen ausschüttete. Und während sie sprachen, konnte Frau Thompson nicht anders, als ein Gefühl der Entschlossenheit in sich aufsteigen zu spüren - ein Wunsch, ihrem Nachbarn auf jede erdenkliche Weise zu helfen.

Und so machte sich Frau Thompson mit einer stählernen Entschlossenheit und einem Funkeln in den Augen auf den Weg in die Stadt, ihr Kopf summte vor Möglichkeiten. Sie besuchte die örtliche Polizeistation, sprach mit den Beamten und lieferte ihnen alle Informationen, die sie über die verschwundene Tochter von Herrn Patel sammeln konnte. Sie verteilte Flyer und sprach mit Nachbarn, um die Gemeinschaft in einer Solidaritäts- und Unterstützungsbekundung zusammenzubringen.

Und als die Tage in Wochen und die Suche nach Herrn Patels Tochter sich erstreckte, weigerte sich Frau Thompson, die Hoffnung aufzugeben. Sie verbrachte ihre Tage und Nächte damit, die Stadt zu durchkämmen, jeder Spur nachzugehen und keinen Stein auf dem anderen zu lassen in ihrem Bestreben, das vermisste Mädchen nach Hause zu bringen.

Und dann, gerade als es schien, als sei alle Hoffnung verloren, erhielt Frau Thompson einen Anruf - einen Anruf, der alles ändern würde. Es war von einer jungen Frau, die behauptete, die Tochter von Herrn Patel auf den Straßen von Manhattan gesehen zu haben, ihr Gesicht blass und ihre Augen vor Angst gefüllt.

Mit einem Gefühl der Dringlichkeit machte sich Frau Thompson auf den Weg in die Nacht, ihr Herz pochte in ihrer Brust, als sie durch die Straßen der Stadt raste. Und dann, gerade als sie aufgeben wollte, erblickte sie eine Gestalt, die sich in der Türöffnung eines verlassenen Gebäudes verkrochen hatte - eine Gestalt, die dem Aussehen nach sehr nach der Tochter von Herrn Patel ähnelte.

Mit einem Freudenschrei stürzte Frau Thompson vorwärts, ihre Arme ausgestreckt, als sie das junge Mädchen in eine warme Umarmung schloss. Und als sie dort im Licht der Straßenlaternen standen, fühlte Frau Thompson eine Erleichterung über sie kommen - ein Gefühl der Erfüllung, das daher rührte, dass sie wusste, dass sie einen Unterschied im Leben eines Menschen gemacht hatte.

Und so führte Frau Thompson Herrn Patels Tochter sicher in ihre Arme zurück zum Brownstone in der Maple Street, wo sich die Gemeinschaft versammelt hatte, um sie mit offenen Armen willkommen zu heißen. Und während sie die ganze Nacht hindurch feierten, Geschichten und Lachen teilten in der warmen Umarmung von Freundschaft und nachbarschaftlicher Liebe, konnte Frau Thompson nicht anders, als ein Gefühl des Stolzes in ihrer kleinen Ecke der Welt zu empfinden - einer Ecke, die mit der Art von Freundlichkeit und Mitgefühl gefüllt war, die New York City zu einem Zuhause machte.

Hope on Broadway

IN THE HEART OF NEW York City, where the towering skyscrapers cast long shadows over the bustling streets below, there existed a world of dreams and despair—a world where the bright lights of Broadway illuminated the stage with tales of love and loss, hope and heartache. This was the realm of the struggling artist, the aspiring actor who chased fame and fortune with a desperation born of necessity, and the streets of Manhattan were their stage, their every move a performance in the grand drama of life.

Among these artists was a young actress named Emily, a starry-eyed ingénue with dreams of stardom and a determination to succeed against all odds. She moved through the city with a grace and elegance that belied her humble origins, her heart filled with a fire that burned brighter than the lights of Times Square.

On a chilly autumn evening, Emily found herself standing outside the stage door of a Broadway theater, her breath forming clouds in the crisp night air. She clutched a faded script in her hand, her heart pounding with anticipation as she waited for her chance to audition for the role of a lifetime.

As she stood there, lost in her thoughts, a voice broke through the silence—a voice belonging to a weary-looking man with a worn-out fedora pulled low over his eyes.

"You here for the audition?" he asked, his tone gruff but not unkind.

Emily nodded, her eyes wide with excitement. "Yes, I am. Are you?"

The man chuckled, a sound like gravel scraping against pavement. "Yeah, something like that. Name's Jake. What about you?"

"Emily," she replied, extending her hand. "Nice to meet you, Jake."

With a nod of acknowledgement, Jake led Emily inside the theater, where the dimly lit corridors echoed with the sounds of footsteps and hushed conversations. They made their way to the audition room, where a panel of stern-faced producers sat behind a long table, their eyes scrutinizing every movement.

Emily took a deep breath and stepped onto the stage, her heart pounding in her chest as she launched into her monologue with a passion and intensity that left the room spellbound. She poured her heart and soul into every word, her voice rising and falling like a symphony of emotion.

And when she was finished, there was a moment of silence—a pregnant pause that hung in the air like a curtain waiting to be drawn. And then, as if on cue, the room erupted into applause, the producers rising to their feet with smiles of approval.

"You've got the part," one of them said, his voice filled with admiration. "Welcome to the cast, Emily."

With tears of joy streaming down her face, Emily turned to Jake, her heart overflowing with gratitude. "Thank you," she whispered, her voice trembling with emotion.

Jake merely nodded, a small smile playing at the corners of his lips. "Don't thank me yet, kid. The hard part's just beginning."

And so, with a mixture of excitement and trepidation, Emily embarked on her journey into the heart of Broadway, her dreams within reach but her future uncertain. She threw herself into rehearsals with a fervor that bordered on obsession, her every waking moment consumed by the relentless pursuit of perfection.

But as the weeks turned into months and the opening night drew near, Emily began to feel the weight of the world bearing down on her shoulders. The pressure to succeed was overwhelming, the expectations of the audience and the critics looming like dark clouds on the horizon.

And then, just when it seemed that all hope was lost, Jake appeared at her side—a beacon of light in the darkness, a voice of reason in a world gone mad.

"You're letting the fear get to you, kid," he said, his voice gentle but firm. "You've got to remember why you're here, what you're fighting for. It's not about the fame or the fortune—it's about the art, the passion, the love of the craft."

With those words ringing in her ears, Emily found the strength to push through her doubts and insecurities, to embrace the magic of the stage and lose herself in the world of make-believe. And when the curtain rose on opening night, she delivered a performance that left the audience breathless, her talent shining like a beacon in the darkness.

As the final curtain fell and the applause rang out like thunder, Emily knew that she had found her place in the world—that she was destined to be a star, not just on Broadway, but in the hearts and minds of all who had witnessed her journey.

And as she stepped out into the night, her heart full and her spirit soaring on the wings of triumph, she knew that no matter what challenges lay ahead, she would face them with the same courage and determination that had brought her to this moment.

Hoffnung am Broadway

IM HERZEN VON NEW YORK City, wo die hoch aufragenden Wolkenkratzer lange Schatten über die belebten Straßen warfen, existierte eine Welt aus Träumen und Verzweiflung - eine Welt, in der die hellen Lichter des Broadways die Bühne mit Geschichten von Liebe und Verlust, Hoffnung und Herzschmerz erleuchteten. Dies war das Reich des kämpfenden Künstlers, des aufstrebenden Schauspielers, der Ruhm und Reichtum mit einer Verzweiflung verfolgte, die aus der Not geboren war, und die Straßen Manhattans waren ihre Bühne, ihre jede Bewegung eine Aufführung im großen Drama des Lebens.

Unter diesen Künstlern war eine junge Schauspielerin namens Emily, eine strahlende Ingenue mit Träumen vom Ruhm und einem Entschluss, gegen alle Widrigkeiten erfolgreich zu sein. Sie bewegte sich mit einer Anmut und Eleganz durch die Stadt, die ihre bescheidenen Ursprünge verbargen, ihr Herz erfüllt von einem Feuer, das heller brannte als die Lichter des Times Square.

An einem kühlen Herbstabend fand sich Emily vor der Bühnentür eines Broadway-Theaters wieder, ihr Atem formte Wolken in der klaren Nachtluft. Sie hielt ein verblasstes Skript in der Hand, ihr Herz klopfte vor Aufregung, während sie auf ihre Chance wartete, für die Rolle ihres Lebens vorzusprechen.

Als sie dort stand, verloren in ihren Gedanken, durchbrach eine Stimme die Stille - eine Stimme, die einem abgekämpft aussehenden Mann mit einem abgenutzten Fedora gehörte, der tief ins Gesicht gezogen war.

"Bist du hier für das Vorsprechen?" fragte er, seine Stimme brummig, aber nicht unfreundlich.

Emily nickte, ihre Augen vor Aufregung weit geöffnet. "Ja, das bin ich. Und du?"

Der Mann lachte, ein Geräusch wie Schotter, der über den Gehweg kratzte. "Ja, so in etwa. Ich heiße Jake. Und du?"

"Emily", antwortete sie und reichte ihm die Hand. "Freut mich, Jake."

Mit einer Nicken der Anerkennung führte Jake Emily in das Theater, wo die schwach beleuchteten Gänge von den Geräuschen von Schritten und gedämpften Gesprächen widerhallten. Sie machten sich auf den Weg zum Vorsprechraum, wo ein Gremium von ernst dreinblickenden Produzenten hinter einem langen Tisch saß, ihre Augen jeden Schritt genau beobachtend.

Emily holte tief Luft und betrat die Bühne, ihr Herz schlug in ihrer Brust, als sie mit einer Leidenschaft und Intensität in ihre Monologe einstieg, die den Raum verzauberte. Sie legte ihr ganzes Herz und ihre Seele in jedes Wort, ihre Stimme stieg und fiel wie eine Symphonie der Emotionen.

Und als sie fertig war, herrschte eine kurze Stille - eine bedeutsame Pause, die in der Luft hing wie ein Vorhang, der darauf wartete, geöffnet zu werden. Und dann, als wäre es ein Signal, brach der Raum in Applaus aus, die Produzenten erhoben sich mit einem anerkennenden Lächeln.

"Du hast die Rolle", sagte einer von ihnen, seine Stimme voller Bewunderung. "Willkommen im Ensemble, Emily."

Mit Freudentränen, die ihr Gesicht hinabströmten, drehte sich Emily zu Jake um, ihr Herz überströmend vor Dankbarkeit. "Danke", flüsterte sie, ihre Stimme vor Emotion zitternd.

Jake nickte nur, ein kleines Lächeln spielte um die Ecken seiner Lippen. "Bedanke dich noch nicht bei mir, Kid. Der schwierige Teil fängt gerade erst an."

Und so begann Emily mit einer Mischung aus Aufregung und Beklommenheit ihre Reise ins Herz des Broadways, ihre Träume zum Greifen nahe, aber ihre Zukunft unsicher. Sie stürzte sich mit einer Leidenschaft, die an Besessenheit grenzte, in die Proben, jeder ihrer wachen Momente war vom rücksichtslosen Streben nach Perfektion erfüllt.

Aber als die Wochen in Monate verstrichen und die Premiere näher rückte, begann Emily, die Last der Welt auf ihren Schultern zu spüren. Der Druck, erfolgreich zu sein, war überwältigend, die Erwartungen des Publikums und der Kritiker wirkten wie dunkle Wolken am Horizont.

Und dann, gerade als es schien, als sei alle Hoffnung verloren, erschien Jake an ihrer Seite - ein Leuchtfeuer im Dunkeln, eine Stimme der Vernunft in einer verrückt gewordenen Welt.

"Du lässt die Angst an dich heran", sagte er, seine Stimme sanft, aber bestimmt. "Du musst dich daran erinnern, warum du hier bist, wofür du kämpfst. Es geht nicht um Ruhm oder Reichtum - es geht um die Kunst, die Leidenschaft, die Liebe zum Handwerk."

Mit diesen Worten im Ohr fand Emily die Kraft, ihre Zweifel und Unsicherheiten zu überwinden, die Magie der Bühne zu umarmen und sich in die Welt der Fantasie zu verlieren. Und als sich der Vorhang zur Eröffnungsnacht hob, lieferte sie eine Performance, die das Publikum atemlos zurückließ, ihr Talent strahlte wie ein Leuchtfeuer in der Dunkelheit.

Als sich der endgültige Vorhang senkte und der Applaus wie Donner erklang, wusste Emily, dass sie ihren Platz in der Welt gefunden hatte - dass sie dazu bestimmt war, nicht nur am Broadway, sondern in den Herzen und Köpfen aller, die ihre Reise miterlebt hatten, ein Stern zu sein.

Und als sie hinaus in die Nacht trat, ihr Herz voll und ihr Geist auf den Flügeln des Triumphs schwebend, wusste sie, dass sie egal vor welchen Herausforderungen sie stehen würde, sie mit dem gleichen Mut und der Entschlossenheit angehen würde, die sie zu diesem Moment gebracht hatten.

Mr. Whiskers

IN THE HEART OF NEW York City, where the skyscrapers towered like giants and the streets thrummed with the energy of a thousand lives intertwined, there existed a peculiar brownstone nestled among the bustling metropolis. This brownstone, with its crooked chimney and ivy-covered walls, was home to the most enigmatic resident of all—a feline of extraordinary intelligence named Mr. Whiskers.

Now, Mr. Whiskers was no ordinary cat. He possessed a keen intellect and a curiosity that bordered on the obsessive, often spending his days exploring the nooks and crannies of the brownstone in search of mysteries to unravel and secrets to uncover.

On a cloudy afternoon, as the rain pattered against the windowpanes and the city bustled below, Mr. Whiskers found himself embroiled in the most perplexing case of his feline career. It all began when his owner, the eccentric Mrs. Pringle, received a letter—a letter that contained a cryptic message written in a language known only to the most cunning of minds.

As Mrs. Pringle puzzled over the mysterious missive, Mr. Whiskers watched with interest, his whiskers twitching with anticipation. He knew that this was no ordinary letter—it was a clue, a clue to a puzzle that would take all of his feline wits to solve.

With a flick of his tail and a determined gleam in his eye, Mr. Whiskers set off into the depths of the brownstone, his nose twitching as he followed the scent of intrigue. He prowled through the dimly lit corridors and dusty attics, his keen senses alert for any sign of danger.

And then, just when he least expected it, Mr. Whiskers stumbled upon a hidden passage—a passage that led to a world of secrets and shadows, a world that few had ever dared to explore.

With a fearless spirit and a sense of adventure that rivaled that of the bravest explorer, Mr. Whiskers ventured deeper into the darkness, his heart pounding with excitement as he followed the twists and turns of the labyrinthine tunnels.

And then, at last, he reached his destination—a hidden chamber filled with ancient artifacts and mysterious symbols, a chamber that held the key to unlocking the secrets of the brownstone once and for all.

With a deft paw and a steady eye, Mr. Whiskers deciphered the cryptic symbols and unraveled the threads of the mystery, revealing a hidden treasure that had been lost to the ages—a treasure that would change the course of history forever.

As he emerged from the depths of the brownstone, the rain still falling softly against the cobblestone streets, Mr. Whiskers knew that he had accomplished something truly remarkable. He had solved the case of the mysterious letter, uncovered the secrets of the hidden chamber, and cemented his place in the annals of feline history as the greatest detective of all time.

And as he curled up on his favorite windowsill, watching the city go by with a satisfied smile on his face, Mr. Whiskers knew that there would always be mysteries to solve and adventures to be had. For in the heart of New York City, where the streets hummed with the rhythm of life and the shadows held untold secrets, there was always another mystery waiting just around the corner—a mystery that only a cat as clever and courageous as Mr. Whiskers could solve.

Mr. Whiskers

IM HERZEN VON NEW YORK City, wo die Wolkenkratzer wie Giganten aufragten und die Straßen vom Puls tausender miteinander verflochtener Leben erfüllt waren, gab es ein eigenartiges Brownstone, das inmitten der geschäftigen Metropole lag. Dieses Brownstone, mit seinem schiefen Schornstein und den von Efeu umrankten Wänden, war die Heimat des rätselhaftesten Bewohners von allen – eines Katers von außergewöhnlicher Intelligenz namens Mr. Whiskers.

Nun, Mr. Whiskers war kein gewöhnlicher Kater. Er besaß einen scharfen Verstand und eine Neugier, die an Obsession grenzte. Oft verbrachte er seine Tage damit, die Winkel und Ecken des Brownstones zu erkunden, auf der Suche nach Rätseln, die es zu lösen und Geheimnissen, die es zu enthüllen galt.

An einem bewölkten Nachmittag, als der Regen gegen die Fensterscheiben prasselte und die Stadt unten pulsierte, fand sich Mr. Whiskers in den verwirrendsten Fall seiner katzenhaften Karriere verwickelt. Alles begann damit, dass seine Besitzerin, die exzentrische Mrs. Pringle, einen Brief erhielt – einen Brief, der eine kryptische Nachricht enthielt, geschrieben in einer Sprache, die nur den gerissensten Geistern bekannt war.

Während Mrs. Pringle über die mysteriöse Mitteilung grübelte, beobachtete Mr. Whiskers interessiert, seine Schnurrhaare zuckten vor Vorfreude. Er wusste, dass dies kein gewöhnlicher Brief war – es war ein Hinweis, ein Hinweis auf ein Rätsel, das all seinen katzenhaften Verstand erfordern würde, um es zu lösen.

Mit einem Schwung seines Schwanzes und einem entschlossenen Funkeln in den Augen machte sich Mr. Whiskers auf in die Tiefen des Brownstones, seine Nase zuckte, als er dem Duft des Rätsels folgte. Er schlich durch die düsteren Korridore und staubigen Dachböden, seine scharfen Sinne auf der Hut vor jeder Gefahr.

Und dann, gerade als er es am wenigsten erwartete, stieß Mr. Whiskers auf einen verborgenen Gang – einen Gang, der zu einer Welt voller Geheimnisse und Schatten führte, einer Welt, die nur wenige je gewagt hatten zu erkunden.

Mit einem furchtlosen Geist und einem Abenteuersinn, der dem mutigsten Entdecker Konkurrenz machte, wagte sich Mr. Whiskers tiefer in die Dunkelheit, sein Herz pochte vor Aufregung, als er den Windungen und Wendungen der labyrinthartigen Tunnel folgte.

Und dann, schließlich, erreichte er sein Ziel – eine verborgene Kammer, gefüllt mit antiken Artefakten und geheimnisvollen Symbolen, eine Kammer, die den Schlüssel dazu enthielt, die Geheimnisse des Brownstones ein für alle Mal zu enthüllen.

Mit einer geschickten Pfote und einem festen Blick entzifferte Mr. Whiskers die kryptischen Symbole und entwirrte die Fäden des Rätsels, und enthüllte einen verborgenen Schatz, der dem Lauf der Geschichte für immer eine andere Richtung geben würde.

Als er aus den Tiefen des Brownstones auftauchte, der Regen immer noch leise gegen die Kopfsteinpflasterstraßen prasselte, wusste Mr. Whiskers, dass er etwas wirklich Bemerkenswertes erreicht hatte. Er hatte den Fall des mysteriösen Briefes gelöst, die Geheimnisse der verborgenen Kammer enthüllt und seinen Platz in den Annalen der katzenhaften Geschichte als der größte Detektiv aller Zeiten besiegelt.

Und als er sich auf seinem Lieblingsfenstersims zusammenrollte und mit einem zufriedenen Lächeln das Treiben der Stadt beobachtete, wusste Mr. Whiskers, dass es immer Rätsel zu lösen und Abenteuer zu erleben geben würde. Denn im Herzen von New York City, wo die Straßen im Rhythmus des Lebens pulsierten und die Schatten unzählige Geheimnisse bargen, gab es immer ein weiteres Rätsel, das nur eine so kluge und mutige Katze wie Mr. Whiskers lösen konnte.

Secrets of Central Park

IN THE HEART OF NEW York City, where the chaos of urban life collided with the tranquility of nature, there existed a world of hidden desires and forbidden passions—a world where the lives of strangers intertwined in the most unexpected of ways, and the secrets buried beneath the surface threatened to unravel the fabric of society itself. This was the realm of Central Park, a verdant oasis amidst the concrete jungle, where the whispers of the wind carried the echoes of a thousand untold stories.

Among the denizens of Central Park was a woman named Grace, a free spirit with a penchant for adventure and a past shrouded in mystery. She moved through the park with the grace of a dancer and the determination of a lioness, her eyes alight with a fire that burned brighter than the midday sun.

On a warm summer afternoon, as the sun dipped low on the horizon and the park was bathed in the golden glow of twilight, Grace found herself wandering through the lush greenery, her senses alive with the sights and sounds of nature. She walked along the winding paths, her footsteps echoing against the pavement like the beat of a distant drum.

As she strolled, lost in her thoughts, Grace stumbled upon a secluded clearing hidden deep within the heart of the park—a place untouched by the hands of man, where the air was thick with the scent of wildflowers and the sounds of the city faded into oblivion.

In the center of the clearing stood a solitary bench, its wooden slats weathered by time and its legs sunk deep into the earth. Grace approached the bench with a sense of reverence, her heart fluttering with anticipation as she took a seat and gazed out at the world beyond.

And then, as if by some twist of fate, she heard a voice—a voice belonging to a man who appeared from the shadows like a ghost from the past.

"Beautiful, isn't it?" he said, his voice soft but filled with a hint of sadness.

Grace turned to see a stranger standing beside her—a man with eyes as blue as the summer sky and a smile that tugged at her heartstrings.

"Yes, it is," she replied, her voice barely above a whisper. "But who are you? And what are you doing here?"

The man chuckled, a sound like the rustle of leaves in the wind. "My name is James, and I come here to escape the chaos of the city—to find solace in the beauty of nature and the peace of solitude."

Grace nodded, her curiosity piqued. "I understand. I come here for the same reason—to find refuge from the noise and the crowds, to lose myself in the serenity of the park."

And so, as the sun dipped below the horizon and the stars began to twinkle in the night sky, Grace and James sat together on the bench, their souls laid bare in the quiet of the evening.

They talked of their hopes and dreams, their fears and regrets, their hearts open like books waiting to be read. And as they spoke, a bond formed between them—a bond that transcended time and space, a connection that defied explanation.

And then, just as the night reached its darkest hour, James leaned in close and whispered three words that would change everything.

"I love you," he said, his voice barely a breath against her ear.

And in that moment, as the world fell away and the secrets of Central Park whispered their approval, Grace knew that she had found something truly extraordinary—a love that was as timeless as the stars themselves.

Geheimnisse des Central Parks

IM HERZEN VON NEW YORK City, wo das Chaos des städtischen Lebens mit der Ruhe der Natur kollidierte, existierte eine Welt verborgener Wünsche und verbotener Leidenschaften – eine Welt, in der sich das Leben von Fremden auf unerwartete Weise verflocht und die Geheimnisse, die unter der Oberfläche verborgen waren, drohten, den Stoff der Gesellschaft selbst zu entwirren. Dies war das Reich des Central Parks, eine üppige Oase mitten im Betondschungel, wo die Flüstern des Windes die Echos von tausend unerzählten Geschichten trugen.

Unter den Bewohnern des Central Parks befand sich eine Frau namens Grace, ein freier Geist mit einer Vorliebe für Abenteuer und einer Vergangenheit, die in Geheimnissen gehüllt war. Sie bewegte sich durch den Park mit der Anmut einer Tänzerin und der Entschlossenheit einer Löwin, ihre Augen leuchteten mit einem Feuer, das heller brannte als die Mittagssonne.

An einem warmen Sommernachmittag, als die Sonne tief am Horizont stand und der Park im goldenen Glanz der Abenddämmerung gebadet wurde, fand sich Grace durch das üppige Grün wandelnd, ihre Sinne lebendig von den Anblicken und Klängen der Natur. Sie schlenderte entlang der gewundenen Pfade, ihre Schritte hallten gegen das Pflaster wie der Klang einer entfernten Trommel.

Während sie in ihren Gedanken versunken war, stolperte Grace über eine abgelegene Lichtung, die tief im Herzen des Parks verborgen lag – ein Ort, der von den Händen des Menschen unberührt war, wo die Luft dick vom Duft der Wildblumen war und die Geräusche der Stadt in Vergessenheit gerieten.

In der Mitte der Lichtung stand eine einsame Bank, ihre hölzernen Latten vom Alter gezeichnet und ihre Beine tief in die Erde versunken. Grace näherte sich der Bank mit Ehrfurcht, ihr Herz flatterte vor Aufregung, als sie Platz nahm und hinausblickte in die Welt.

Und dann, als ob es durch eine Laune des Schicksals geschah, hörte sie eine Stimme – eine Stimme, die einem Mann gehörte, der aus den Schatten auftauchte wie ein Geist aus der Vergangenheit.

"Schön, nicht wahr?" sagte er, seine Stimme sanft, aber mit einem Hauch von Traurigkeit.

Grace drehte sich um und sah einen Fremden neben sich stehen – einen Mann mit Augen so blau wie der Sommerhimmel und einem Lächeln, das an ihren Herzsträngen zog.

"Ja, das ist es", antwortete sie, ihre Stimme kaum mehr als ein Flüstern. "Aber wer bist du? Und was machst du hier?"

Der Mann lachte leise, ein Klang wie das Rascheln von Blättern im Wind. "Mein Name ist James, und ich komme hierher, um dem Chaos der Stadt zu entfliehen – um Trost in der Schönheit der Natur und dem Frieden der Einsamkeit zu finden."

Grace nickte, ihre Neugierde geweckt. "Ich verstehe. Ich komme aus demselben Grund hierher – um Zuflucht vor dem Lärm und den Menschenmassen zu finden, um mich in der Ruhe des Parks zu verlieren."

Und so, als die Sonne unter dem Horizont versank und die Sterne am Nachthimmel zu funkeln begannen, saßen Grace und James gemeinsam auf der Bank, ihre Seelen in der Stille des Abends ausgebreitet.

Sie sprachen von ihren Hoffnungen und Träumen, ihren Ängsten und Bedauern, ihre Herzen offen wie Bücher, die darauf warteten, gelesen zu werden. Und während sie sprachen, entstand eine Bindung zwischen ihnen – eine Bindung, die Zeit und Raum überdauerte, eine Verbindung, die jede Erklärung trotzte.

Und dann, gerade als die Nacht ihre dunkelste Stunde erreichte, lehnte sich James nah heran und flüsterte drei Worte, die alles verändern würden.

"Ich liebe dich", sagte er, seine Stimme kaum mehr als ein Hauch in ihrem Ohr.

Und in diesem Moment, als die Welt verschwand und die Geheimnisse des Central Parks ihre Zustimmung flüsterten, wusste Grace, dass sie etwas wirklich Außergewöhnliches gefunden hatte – eine Liebe, die so zeitlos war wie die Sterne selbst.

Tales from the Upper West Side

IN THE HEART OF NEW York City, where the streets hummed with the rhythm of life and the brownstones stood like silent sentinels guarding the secrets of their inhabitants, there existed a world of quiet charm and gentle humor—a world where the lives of ordinary people intersected in the most delightful of ways, and the simplest of moments held the promise of unexpected joy. This was the realm of the Upper West Side, a neighborhood rich in history and character, where the quirks and eccentricities of its residents were celebrated rather than shunned.

Among the denizens of the Upper West Side was a woman named Claire, a retired librarian with a love for crossword puzzles and a knack for getting into amusing predicaments. She lived alone in a cozy apartment on the fourth floor of a brownstone, her days filled with leisurely strolls through Central Park and impromptu visits to the local bakery.

On a sunny morning, as the aroma of freshly brewed coffee filled her apartment and the sounds of the city drifted in through the open window, Claire found herself embarking on a most unexpected adventure. It all began when she received a letter—a letter that contained an invitation to a mysterious event taking place in a hidden corner of Central Park.

Intrigued, Claire donned her favorite hat and set off into the park, her curiosity piqued and her imagination running wild. She followed the directions in the letter, winding her way through the labyrinthine paths until she reached a secluded glade bathed in dappled sunlight.

And there, waiting for her amidst the trees, was a most curious sight—a gathering of strangers, each one dressed in elaborate costumes and bearing gifts of food and drink.

"Welcome, dear lady," said a gentleman with a twinkle in his eye, his voice warm and inviting. "We are the Society of Eccentric Souls, and we have been expecting you."

Claire blinked in surprise, her eyes widening with wonder. "But how did you know I would come?"

The gentleman chuckled, a sound like the tinkling of wind chimes on a summer breeze. "We have our ways, my dear. But enough about that—come, join us in our revelry. There is much to celebrate!"

And so, with a sense of excitement bubbling in her chest, Claire joined the Society of Eccentric Souls in their merry-making, feasting on delicacies and dancing beneath the stars until the wee hours of the morning.

As the night wore on and the laughter echoed through the trees, Claire found herself drawn to a man with a mischievous glint in his eye—a man named Henry, who regaled her with tales of his adventures in far-off lands and his encounters with colorful characters.

And as they danced together beneath the moonlit sky, Claire felt a sense of joy wash over her—a feeling of belonging that she had never experienced before. For in the company of the Society of Eccentric Souls, she had found kindred spirits who embraced her quirks and celebrated her eccentricities, a family of strangers bound together by the bonds of friendship and a shared love of the absurd.

And so, as the first light of dawn began to creep over the horizon and the Society of Eccentric Souls bid farewell to their magical gathering, Claire knew that she had stumbled upon something truly extraordinary—a community of kindred spirits who had welcomed her into their midst with open arms, a world of laughter and love hidden in the heart of the city that never sleeps.

Geschichten aus der Upper West Side

IM HERZEN VON NEW YORK City, wo die Straßen mit dem Rhythmus des Lebens summten und die Brownstones wie stille Wächter standen, die die Geheimnisse ihrer Bewohner hüteten, existierte eine Welt von ruhigem Charme und sanftem Humor - eine Welt, in der sich das Leben gewöhnlicher Menschen auf die herrlichste Weise kreuzte und die einfachsten Momente das Versprechen unerwarteter Freude bargen. Dies war das Reich der Upper West Side, einer Nachbarschaft reich an Geschichte und Charakter, in der die Eigenheiten und Exzentrik ihrer Bewohner gefeiert wurden, anstatt verpönt zu sein.

Unter den Bewohnern der Upper West Side war eine Frau namens Claire, eine pensionierte Bibliothekarin mit einer Vorliebe für Kreuzworträtsel und einem Talent, in amüsante Zwangslagen zu geraten. Sie lebte allein in einer gemütlichen Wohnung im vierten Stock eines Brownstones, ihre Tage waren gefüllt mit gemütlichen Spaziergängen durch den Central Park und spontanen Besuchen in der örtlichen Bäckerei.

An einem sonnigen Morgen, als der Duft von frisch gebrühtem Kaffee ihre Wohnung erfüllte und die Geräusche der Stadt durch das offene Fenster hereinwehten, machte sich Claire auf zu einem äußerst unerwarteten Abenteuer. Alles begann, als sie einen Brief erhielt - einen Brief, der eine Einladung zu einer geheimnisvollen Veranstaltung enthielt, die an einem versteckten Ort im Central Park stattfinden sollte.

Intrigiert zog Claire ihren Lieblingshut auf und machte sich auf in den Park, ihre Neugierde geweckt und ihre Fantasie tobend. Sie folgte den Anweisungen im Brief und schlängelte sich durch die labyrinthartigen Pfade, bis sie eine abgelegene Lichtung erreichte, die in von der Sonne gefiltertem Licht gebadet war.

Und dort, sie erwartend zwischen den Bäumen, war ein äußerst merkwürdiger Anblick - eine Versammlung von Fremden, von denen jeder in aufwändigen Kostümen gekleidet war und Geschenke von Essen und Trinken mitbrachte.

"Willkommen, liebe Dame", sagte ein Herr mit einem Zwinkern in den Augen, seine Stimme warm und einladend. "Wir sind die Gesellschaft der exzentrischen Seelen, und wir haben dich erwartet."

Claire blinzelte überrascht, ihre Augen weiteten sich vor Staunen. "Aber wie wusstet ihr, dass ich kommen würde?"

Der Herr lachte leise, ein Klang wie das Klingeln von Windspielen in einer Sommerbrise. "Wir haben unsere Wege, meine Liebe. Aber genug davon - komm, schließ dich uns in unserem Fest an. Es gibt viel zu feiern!"

Und so schloss sich Claire mit einem Gefühl der Aufregung in ihrer Brust der Gesellschaft der exzentrischen Seelen in ihrem fröhlichen Treiben an, schmauste von Köstlichkeiten und tanzte bis in die frühen Morgenstunden unter den Sternen.

Während die Nacht verging und das Gelächter durch die Bäume hallte, fühlte sich Claire zu einem Mann mit einem schelmischen Glanz in den Augen hingezogen - einem Mann namens Henry, der sie mit Geschichten von seinen Abenteuern in fernen Ländern und seinen Begegnungen mit bunten Charakteren unterhielt.

Und als sie gemeinsam unter dem von Mondlicht erhellten Himmel tanzten, fühlte Claire eine tiefe Freude in sich aufsteigen - ein Gefühl des Zugehörigseins, das sie zuvor nie erlebt hatte. Denn in der Gesellschaft der exzentrischen Seelen hatte sie Gleichgesinnte gefunden, die ihre Eigenheiten begrüßten und ihre Exzentrik feierten, eine Familie von Fremden, die durch die Bande der Freundschaft und der geteilten Liebe zum Absurden verbunden waren.

Und so, als das erste Licht der Morgendämmerung begann, über den Horizont zu kriechen und die Gesellschaft der exzentrischen Seelen sich von ihrer magischen Versammlung verabschiedete, wusste Claire, dass sie auf etwas wirklich Außergewöhnliches gestoßen war - eine Gemeinschaft von Gleichgesinnten, die sie mit offenen Armen in ihre Mitte aufgenommen hatte, eine Welt des Lachens und der Liebe, verborgen im Herzen der Stadt, die niemals schläft.

www.ingramcontent.com/pod-product-compliance
Lightning Source LLC
Chambersburg PA
CBHW071358130726
47996CB00002B/986